Illustrated by Sally Kindberg

Photography by Peter Anderson,
Geoff Brightling, Philip Dowell,
Neil Fletcher, Frank Greenaway,
Alan Hills, Barnabas Kindersley,
Dave King, Karl Shone, Jerry Young

The publisher would like to thank the
following for their kind permission to
reproduce their photographs:
a = above, c = centre, b = below/bottom,
l = left, r = right, t = top.

Cold
Ace Photo Agency: Peter Adams 3b, 5bl;
Robert Harding Picture Library: 11tl;
Images Colour Library: 4–5; **Tony Stone
Images:** John Edwards 11b; David E.
Myers 6–7; Michael Townsend 8l.

Gatefold
Tony Stone Images: John Edwards br;
High Sitton bl; Michael Townsend tcr.

Hot
The J. Allan Cash Photolibrary: 8l, 9c;
Robert Harding Picture Library: Gavin
Hellier 5br; Geoff Renner 3b; **Pictor
International:** 4–5, 10l; **Spectrum Colour
Library:** 11 tl; **Tony Stone Images:** James
Strachan 10–11; **Telegraph Colour
Library:** Terry Carew 7 bl.

Jacket
Images Colour Library: iceberg;
Pictor International: desert.

Contents

4 Polar lands

6 Polar animals

8 Tiny plants

10 People at the Poles

Cold index

animals 4, 6
Antarctica 4
Arctic 5, 8, 10, 11
Arctic willow 9
boots 10
burrow 7
clothes 10
dog sledge 11
egg 6
emperor penguin 6
flower 8, 9
fur 7
grass 8, 9
house 10
husky dog 11

ice 4, 5, 6, 7, 8, 11
iceberg 5
insect 9
kayak 11
lemming 7
moss 7, 8
North Pole 5
northern fleabane 9
northern primrose 9
ocean 5
penguin 4, 6
people 10, 11
plant 8, 9
polar bear 7
polar lands 4

Poles 10
reindeer 7
sea 4, 5, 11
seal 11
seed 9
snow 6, 7, 10
snowmobile 11
South Pole 4
summer 5, 8, 11
tree 9
wind 4, 9
winter 9
wolf 7

COLD

Explore the amazing world of polar lands

Claire Llewellyn

London • New York • Sydney • Moscow • Delhi

Polar lands are cold, icy places with biting winds.

Land of ice

Antarctica is a frozen land covered by thick sheets of ice near the South Pole. It is the coldest, windiest place in the world.

Thick feathers keep penguins warm in the sea.

At home in the cold

Polar animals live a difficult life, but have special ways of beating the cold.

4

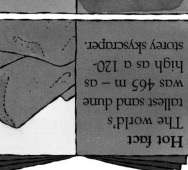

Cold fact
The world's tallest iceberg was 167 m – as high as a 40-storey building.

Hot fact
The world's tallest sand dune was 465 m – as high as a 120-storey skyscraper.

Frozen sea

The Arctic is a huge frozen ocean near the North Pole. The ice slowly melts during the warmer summer months.

Polar animals survive in the freezing ice and snow.

Egg cosy

An emperor penguin's egg never touches the icy ground. The male keeps the egg warm on his feet.

The male penguin tucks the egg under a warm flap of skin.

Moss muncher

Reindeer scrape away the ice with their hooves and feed on the moss below.

Cold fact
Lemmings dig warm burrows under the snow to take shelter from the cold.

Hot fact
Elf owls live in shady holes inside desert cacti to keep out of the sun.

Warm furs

Polar bears have a thick layer of fat just under the skin and a cosy fur coat to keep out the cold.

White hunter

A hungry wolf is hidden by its snow-white coat of fur.

7

Tiny plants grow when the ice melts away.

Arctic summer colour
A colourful blanket of grasses, mosses, and pretty wild flowers grows in the summer sun.

Flower cushion

Some plants trap a little water and warmth by growing together in low, round clumps.

The northern fleabane has daisy-like flowers.

Out of the wind

Only tough plants can survive the icy winters. This grass grows low to keep out of the wind.

Look at me!

The northern primrose's large, bright flower is a draw for any passing insect. Visiting insects help the plant to make new seeds.

People at the Poles wear **warm**, winter clothes

House on legs
The wooden houses in the Arctic are built on stilts to keep above the snow.

Layers of clothing trap in body heat.

Head to toe
Thick boots, padded clothes, and cosy, fur hoods keep Arctic people warm in the freezing snow.

10

Cool flowers

Arctic plants flower in the cool summer months when the frozen soil thaws.

Cool

Cold

Mosquito madness

Swarms of mosquitoes hatch in the Arctic summer and drive the poor reindeer mad.

Skating on ice

Inuit children play ice hockey in winter when the ice is frozen hard.

Hunting boat

Arctic people hunt for seals when the frozen sea melts in summer. They travel in speedy kayaks made of wood.

Cold fact
A snowmobile is today's way of travelling long distances over the ice.

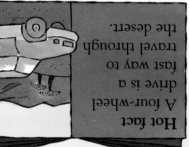

Hot fact
A four-wheel drive is a fast way to travel through the desert.

Animal power

A dog sledge is a good way to travel on the ice. Husky dogs are hardy, strong, and fast!

Shivering chicks

Emperor penguin chicks hatch in
the freezing winter weather.
Their woolly coats keep
them warm.

Very cold   Freezing cold

Instant ice

The coldest polar temperature ever was –89.2° C.
This would turn boiling water instantly to ice.

Could a lizard survive at the cold Poles?

No. The lizard would be too cold to move. It would be easy prey for other animals.

Lift the flaps to see the differences between cold and hot lands.

Could a polar bear live in the hot desert?

No. The polar bear would overheat in its furry coat and very soon collapse.

Lift the flaps to compare life in deserts with life in polar lands.

Desert market

In the desert, food is hard to grow. People travel many miles to buy and sell goods at the busy market.

Outdoor life

These children live in the hottest, driest part of Australia. The sun shines here all the year round.

11

Desert people take shelter from the hot sun.

A headcloth keeps off sand.

Shady homes

Desert homes are shady and cool. They have thick walls to keep out the heat of the sun.

Tiny windows let in less heat.

Cool clothes

Long, loose clothes are cool in the day but warm at night.

10

Juicy
cactus
stem

Bunches of
delicious
dates grow
on the trees.

Hot fact
The whisker
cactus opens its
flowers at night
to attract
feeding moths.

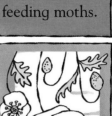

Cold fact
Arctic poppies
open in the
morning and
swivel round to
follow the sun.

Desert tree
Palm trees can only grow in the
sandy soil of an oasis. This is a
place in the desert
with water
underground.

Rotten rose
The desert rose is
pretty but poisonous.
Animals leave it alone.

Tall, **prickly** cacti grow in **parched,** **rocky** ground.

Water storer
A saguaro cactus slurps up water and stores it in its fat, fleshy stems.

Tiny spines

Waxy leaves lock in water.

Don't eat me!
Many desert plants have sharp spines. These help to keep thirsty animals away from their juicy stems.

A sting in the tail

A scorpion hunts in the cool of the night. It kills spiders with its poisonous sting.

Sting

Sharp claws

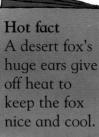

Hot fact A desert fox's huge ears give off heat to keep the fox nice and cool.

Cold fact
An Arctic fox's ears are small to stop the fox from losing body warmth.

Furry disguise

A gerbil's sandy-coloured fur helps it to hide on moonlit nights.

On the lookout

At the first sign of danger, meerkats dive into their shady burrows.

Desert creatures burrow in the soft scorching sand

A deadly bite

The poisonous sand viper hides in the sand waiting for its prey. It pounces on lizards and rats.

A few quick wriggles in the soft sand ...

... and the snake is almost out of sight.

Sandy land

The Sahara Desert in North Africa is like a rolling sea of sand. It is the hottest place in the world. The days are burning hot, but the nights are freezing cold.

Stony land

Not all deserts have sand dunes. This North American desert is covered with dry stones and bare rock.

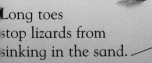
Long toes stop lizards from sinking in the sand.

Deserts are hot, dry places tha sizzle in the sun.

Long legs keep a camel's body high off the hot sand.

Home sweet home?
Many animals manage to live in the hot desert, but it's a harsh, uncomfortable home.

HOT

Discover the amazing world of deserts

Claire Llewellyn

London • New York • Sydney • Moscow • Delhi

www.dk.com

Editor Jane Yorke
Senior Editor Mary Atkinson
Senior Art Editor Chris Scollen
Art Editor Mary Sandberg
DTP Designer Phil Keeble
Production Josie Alabaster
Jacket Design Helen Melville
Picture Research Jamie Robinson
and Lee Thompson

Published in Great Britain by
Dorling Kindersley Limited,
9 Henrietta Street,
London WC2E 8PS

2 4 6 8 10 9 7 5 3 1

A CIP catalogue record for this book is available
from the British Library.

ISBN: 0-7513-5847-9

Colour reproduction by Colourscan, Singapore
Printed and bound in Italy by L.E.G.O.

Contents

4 Deserts

6 Desert creatures

8 Tall, prickly cacti

10 Desert people

Hot index

animal 4, 8, 9
Australia 11
Bedouin 11
burrow 7
cactus 8, 9
camel 4
children 11
clothes 10
creature 6
date 9
desert 4, 5, 11
desert fox 7
desert rose 9
flowers 9
food 11

gerbil 7
headcloth 10
home 4, 10
lizard 5, 6
market 11
meerkat 7
moth 9
North Africa 5
North America 5
oasis 9
palm tree 9
people 10, 11
plant 8
rat 6
rock 5

saguaro cactus 8
Sahara Desert 5
sand 4, 5, 6, 10
sand dune 5
sandstorm 5
sand viper 6
scorpion 7
snake 6
spider 7
stone 5
sun 4, 10, 11
tent 11
water 8, 9
whisker cactus 9